W9-AMN-029

Healthy Eating with MyPlate

Using MyPlate

Rebecca Rissman

Heinemann
LIBRARY

Chicago, Illinois

www.capstonepub.com
Visit our website to find out more information about Heinemann-Raintree books.

To order:
☎ Phone 888-454-2279

🖥 Visit www.capstonepub.com to browse our catalog and order online.

Edited by Rebecca Rissman, Catherine Veitch, and Adrian Vigliano
Designed by Joanna Hinton-Malivoire
Picture research by Elizabeth Alexander
Production by Victoria Fitzgerald
Originated by Capstone Global Library Ltd
Printed in the United States of America by Worzalla Publishing.

15 14 13 12 11
10 9 8 7 6 5 4 3 2 1

Library of Congress Cataloging-in-Publication Data
Cataloging-in-Publication data is on file at the Library of Congress.

ISBN: 978-1-4329-6978-3 (HC) 978-1-4329-6985-1 (PB)

Acknowledgments
We would like to thank the following for permission to reproduce photographs: © Capstone Publishers pp. 6, 7, 7, 7, 7, 9, 17, 19, 20, 23 top, 23 middle (Karon Dubke); Alamy p. 16 (© Tetra Images); Getty Images p. 5 (Jupiterimages/Brand X Pictures); Photolibrary p. 12 (John Smith/Fancy); Shutterstock pp. 4 (© Monkey Business Images), 8, 10 (© happykanppy), 11 (© Marie C Fields), 13 (© Anna Kucherova), 14 (© Valentyn Volkov), 15 (© Morgan Lane Photography), 18 (© Magone), 21 (© Giovanna - ricordi fotografici), 23 bottom (© Morgan Lane Photography); U.S. Department of Agriculture, Center for Nutrition Policy and Promotion p. 8 inset.

Front and back cover photograph of boy looking at MyPlate poster reproduced with the permission of © Capstone Publishers (Karon Dubke). MyPlate image courtesy of U.S. Department of Agriculture, Center for Nutrition Policy and Promotion

Every effort has been made to contact copyright holders of material reproduced in this book. Any omissions will be rectified in subsequent printings if notice is given to the publishers.

Contents

Stay Healthy

It is important to stay healthy.

Staying healthy means being fit and eating well.

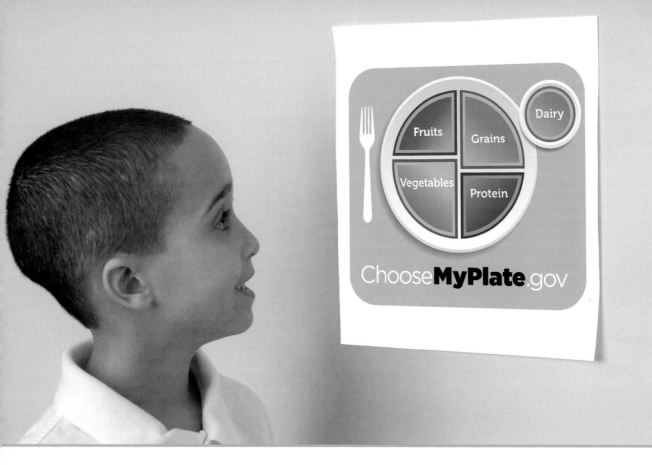

MyPlate reminds us how to eat well.

grains

fruit

vegetables

dairy

protein

MyPlate shows us the five
food groups.

MyPlate looks like a dinner plate and
a glass of milk.

This is to remind us to stay healthy at every meal.

Vegetables

MyPlate reminds us to eat
many vegetables.

Carrots, onions, and radishes are types of vegetables.

Fruits

MyPlate reminds us to eat fruits, too.

Bananas, pineapples, and kiwis are types of fruits.

Grains

MyPlate reminds us to eat
many grains.

Pasta, bread, and rice are types
of grains.

Protein

MyPlate reminds us to eat protein, too.

Foods such as chicken, beef, pork, fish, and beans give us protein.

17

Dairy

MyPlate reminds us to drink milk or eat other dairy foods.

Dairy foods are made from milk.

Cheese and yogurt are dairy foods.

Filling Your Plate

MyPlate shows us to fill half our plates with fruits and vegetables.

MyPlate shows us to eat some protein, grains, and dairy, too.

Remember!

- Half the grains you eat should be made from whole grains.

- Eat lean protein.

- Eat different types of fruits and vegetables.

- Eat low fat dairy foods.

Picture Glossary

healthy fit and well

lean low in fat. Lean protein is a healthy food to eat.

whole grains whole seeds from some plants used in foods. Foods made with whole grains are good for you.

Index

Notes to Parents and Teachers

Before Reading
Tell children that eating healthy foods helps people to stay well. Explain that there are different food groups that contain different types of healthy foods. Write the five food groups on the board: protein, fruits, vegetables, dairy, and grains.

After Reading
• Place children into five groups, and assign each group one food group. Ask each group to make a list of different foods in that group. Then have each group report back to the class all the foods they listed.

WITHDRAWN